# Mules Rule

Written by Michèle Dufresne

PIONEER VALLEY EDUCATIONAL PRESS, INC.

Here is a mule.

A mule is a mix of a **horse**

and a **donkey**.

Mules have long **ears** like a donkey.

They have strong legs like a horse.

They come in lots of sizes.

George Washington used mules on his farm. He found that mules can work longer and harder than horses.

Mules use their strong legs
to push and pull big things.
You can pack things
on a mule's back.

On this June day, one mule is going to help move all these big logs.

Mules are cute.

They have soft manes.

But look out!

A mule will kick if you make it mad.

Mules are usually quite calm and patient, but when they get angry, they can kick both sideways and backward. Do not stand behind a mule!

Mules are not mute.

They can make **sounds**.

They can sound like a horse,

and they can sound like a donkey.

A mule can make a whinnying sound like a horse or a braying sound like a donkey to communicate its feelings. A mule can also whimper when it's excited or worried.

Mules are **smart**.

They keep you safe

when you ride them.

Mules are very intelligent. They know how to be careful and will refuse to do something that might put them in danger.

Some trained mules are used in wilderness search and rescue missions because of their stamina and ability to navigate tough terrain.

# glossary

**donkey:**
a small animal with long ears that is strong and can carry heavy loads

**ears:**
body parts on the head that help animals hear

**horse:**
a large animal with a long tail that can run fast and pull loads

**smart:**
able to learn and understand things quickly

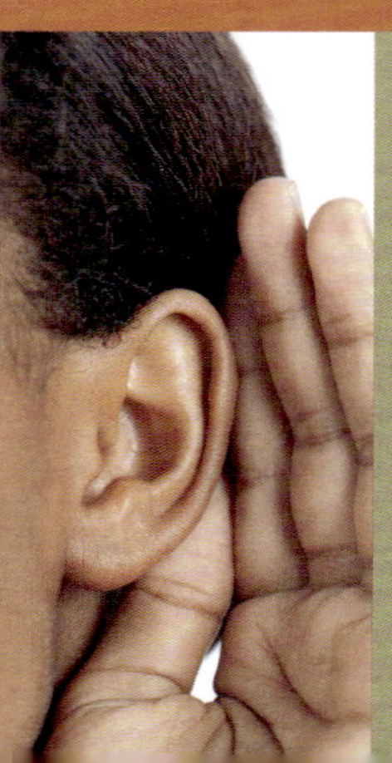

**sounds:**
noises that can be heard